Pebble™ Plus

Healthy Eating with MyPyramid

The Vegetable Group

by Mari C. Schuh

Consulting Editor: Gail Saunders-Smith, PhD

Consultant: Barbara J. Rolls, PhD
Guthrie Chair in Nutrition
The Pennsylvania State University
University Park, Pennsylvania

Capstone
press
Mankato, Minnesota

Pebble Plus is published by Capstone Press,
151 Good Counsel Drive, P.O. Box 669, Mankato, Minnesota 56002.
www.capstonepress.com

1 2 3 4 5 6 11 10 09 08 07 06

Library of Congress Cataloging-in-Publication Data
Schuh, Mari C., 1975–
    The vegetable group / by Mari C. Schuh.
    p. cm.—(Pebble plus. Healthy eating with MyPyramid)
    Summary: "Simple text and photographs present the vegetable group, the foods in this group,
and examples of healthy eating choices"—Provided by publisher.
    Includes bibliographical references and index.
    ISBN-13: 978-0-7368-5374-3 (hardcover)
    ISBN-10: 0-7368-5374-X (hardcover)
    ISBN-13: 978-0-7368-6928-7 (softcover pbk.)
    ISBN-10: 0-7368-6928-X (softcover pbk.)
    1. Vegetables—Juvenile literature. 2. Nutrition—Juvenile literature. I. Title. II. Series.
TX557.S38 2006
641.3'5—dc22   2005023427

Credits
Jennifer Bergstrom, designer; Kelly Garvin, photo researcher; Stacy Foster and Michelle Biedscheid,
    photo shoot coordinators

Photo Credits
BananaStock Ltd., 1; Capstone Press/Karon Dubke, cover, 3, 5, 9, 11, 13, 15, 16–17, 18–19, 21, 22 (all);
Corbis/Andreas von Einsiedel/Elizabeth Whiting & Associates, 15 (background), 19 (background); Corbis/
Ariel Skelley, 6–7; Getty Images Inc./Patti McConville, 5 (background), 21 (background); U.S. Department
of Agriculture, 8, 9 (inset)

The author dedicates this book to Mapleton librarian Bonnie Klein and her husband, Karl, whose vegetable
garden is larger than the library where she works.

**Information in this book supports the U.S. Department of Agriculture's MyPyramid for Kids
food guidance system found at http://www.MyPyramid.gov/kids. Food amounts listed in this
book are based on an 1,800-calorie food plan.**

**The U.S. Department of Agriculture (USDA) does not endorse any products, services,
or organizations.**

Note to Parents and Teachers

The Healthy Eating with MyPyramid set supports national science standards related to
nutrition and physical health. This book describes and illustrates the vegetable group.
The images support early readers in understanding the text. The repetition of words and
phrases helps early readers learn new words. This book also introduces early readers
to subject-specific vocabulary words, which are defined in the Glossary section. Early
readers may need assistance to read some words and to use the Table of Contents,
Glossary, Read More, Internet Sites, and Index sections of the book.

Table of Contents

Vegetables

How many vegetables

have you eaten today?

Did you know that vegetables come from plants? Vegetables help keep you healthy and strong.

MyPyramid for Kids

MyPyramid teaches you
how much to eat
from each food group.
Vegetables are one
food group in MyPyramid.

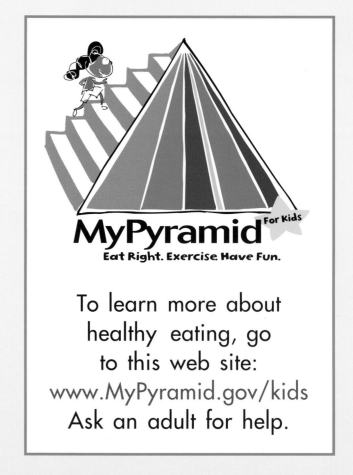

MyPyramid For Kids

Eat Right. Exercise. Have Fun.

To learn more about
healthy eating, go
to this web site:
www.MyPyramid.gov/kids
Ask an adult for help.

Kids should eat
at least 2½ cups
of vegetables every day.

Enjoying Vegetables

Cucumbers, carrots, cabbage.

There are all kinds

of vegetables.

If you don't like one,

try another.

13

Yellow, red, green.

See how many colors

you can eat.

Corn, tomatoes, and lettuce

are part of a healthy meal.

Crunch, crunch, crunch.

Carrots and celery

make a fun snack.

You can make

a vegetable pizza.

Top it with peppers

and mushrooms.

Vegetables are part
of a healthy meal.
What are your
favorite vegetables?

How Much to Eat

Kids need to eat at least 2½ cups of vegetables every day. To get 2½ cups, pick five of your favorite vegetables below.

Pick five of your favorite vegetables to eat today!

½ cup broccoli   ½ cup carrots   ½ cup vegetable juice   ½ cup corn

½ baked potato   ½ cup cucumbers   ½ cup tomatoes   ½ cup green beans

½ cup + ½ cup + ½ cup + ½ cup + ½ cup = 2½ cups

Healthy Eating with MyPyramid

The Milk Group

by Mari C. Schuh

Consulting Editor: Gail Saunders-Smith, PhD

Consultant: Barbara J. Rolls, PhD
Guthrie Chair in Nutrition
The Pennsylvania State University
University Park, Pennsylvania

Capstone
press
Mankato, Minnesota

Pebble Plus is published by Capstone Press,
151 Good Counsel Drive, P.O. Box 669, Mankato, Minnesota 56002.
www.capstonepress.com

1 2 3 4 5 6 11 10 09 08 07 06

Library of Congress Cataloging-in-Publication Data
Schuh, Mari C., 1975–
    The milk group / by Mari C. Schuh.
    p. cm.—(Healthy eating with MyPyramid)
    Summary: "Simple text and photographs present the milk group, the foods in this group, and examples of
healthy eating choices"—Provided by publisher.
    Includes bibliographical references and index.
    ISBN-13: 978-0-7368-5373-6 (hardcover)
    ISBN-10: 0-7368-5373-1 (hardcover)
    ISBN-13: 978-0-7368-6925-6 (softcover pbk.)
    ISBN-10: 0-7368-6925-5 (softcover pbk.)
    1. Dairy products—Juvenile literature. 2. Nutrition—Juvenile literature. I. Title.
TX377.S38 2006
641.3'7—dc22   2005023699

Credits
Jennifer Bergstrom, designer; Kelly Garvin, photo researcher; Stacy Foster and Michelle Biedscheid,
        photo shoot coordinators

Photo Credits
Capstone Press/Karon Dubke, cover, 3, 5, 6–7, 9, 11, 12–13, 15, 16–17, 19, 21, 22 (all)
Getty Images Inc./Seymour Hewitt, 1
U.S. Department of Agriculture, 8, 9 (inset)

The author dedicates this book to Joseph Quam of Byron, Minnesota.

Capstone Press thanks Hilltop Hy-Vee employees in Mankato, Minnesota, for their helpful assistance with
photo shoots.

**Information in this book supports the U.S. Department of Agriculture's MyPyramid for Kids
food guidance system found at http://www.MyPyramid.gov/kids. Food amounts listed in this
book are based on an 1,800-calorie food plan.**

**The U.S. Department of Agriculture (USDA) does not endorse any products, services,
or organizations.**

Note to Parents and Teachers

The Healthy Eating with MyPyramid set supports national science standards related to
nutrition and physical health. This book describes and illustrates the milk group. The
images support early readers in understanding the text. The repetition of words and
phrases helps early readers learn new words. This book also introduces early readers
to subject-specific vocabulary words, which are defined in the Glossary section. Early
readers may need assistance to read some words and to use the Table of Contents,
Glossary, Read More, Internet Sites, and Index sections of the book.

Table of Contents

The Milk Group

Milk, cheese, yogurt.

How many dairy products

have you had today?

5

Foods in the milk group

have calcium.

Your bones and teeth

need calcium to grow

healthy and strong.

MyPyramid for Kids

MyPyramid teaches you
how much to eat
from each food group.
The milk group is
part of MyPyramid.

MyPyramid For Kids

Eat Right. Exercise. Have Fun.

To learn more about
healthy eating, go
to this web site:
www.MyPyramid.gov/kids
Ask an adult for help.

9

Kids should eat
and drink 3 cups
from the milk group
every day.

11

Enjoying the Milk Group

Wow! Look at all the kinds of milk. Choose low-fat milk and low-fat dairy foods.

White, pink, brown.

If you don't like white milk,

try chocolate or strawberry.

Which one is your favorite?

15

Sweet, smooth, and creamy.

Dip fruit in your yogurt

for a tasty treat.

Hard, soft,

yellow, or white.

Find many kinds

of low-fat cheese

at your grocery store.

The milk group is

a part of a healthy meal.

What are your favorite foods

made from milk?

How Much to Eat

Most kids need to have 3 cups from the milk group every day. To get 3 cups, pick three of your favorite milk products below.

Pick three of your favorite milk products to enjoy today!

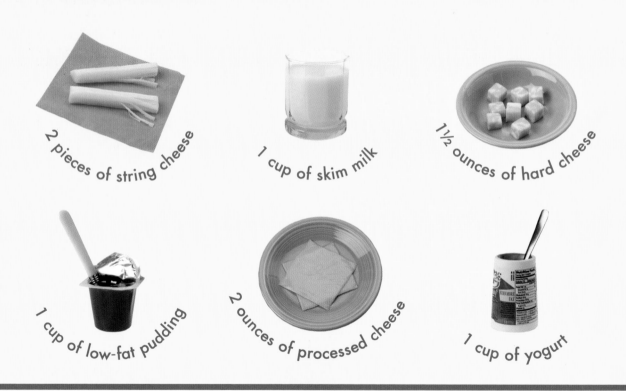

2 pieces of string cheese

1 cup of skim milk

1½ ounces of hard cheese

1 cup of low-fat pudding

2 ounces of processed cheese

1 cup of yogurt

1 cup + 1 cup + 1 cup = 3 cups

Glossary

calcium—a mineral that the body uses to build teeth and bones

dairy—foods that are made with milk; milk, cheese, and yogurt are kinds of dairy foods.

MyPyramid—a food plan that helps kids make healthy food choices and reminds kids to be active; MyPyramid was made by the U.S. Department of Agriculture.

Read More

Klingel, Cynthia Fitterer, and Robert B. Noyed. *Milk and Cheese.* Let's Read About Food. Milwaukee: Weekly Reader Early Learning Library, 2002.

Nelson, Robin. *Dairy.* First Step Nonfiction. Minneapolis: Lerner, 2003.

Rondeau, Amanda. *Milk Is Magnificant.* What Should I Eat? Edina, Minn.: Abdo, 2003.

Index

Word Count: 142
Grade: 1
Early-Intervention Level: 14

Internet Sites

FactHound offers a safe, fun way to find Internet sites related to this book. All of the sites on FactHound have been researched by our staff.

Here's how:

1. Visit *www.facthound.com*

2. Type in this special code **0736853731** for age-appropriate sites. Or enter a search word related to this book for a more general search.

3. Click on the **Fetch It** button.

FactHound will fetch the best sites for you!